ENVIRONMENTAL DISASTERS

Chernobyl

Nuclear Disaster

by Nichol Bryan

WORLD ALMANAC® LIBRARY

Please visit our web site at: www.worldalmanaclibrary.com
For a free color catalog describing World Almanac® Library's list of high-quality books
and multimedia programs, call 1-800-848-2928 (USA) or 1-800-387-3178 (Canada).
World Almanac® Library's fax: (414) 332-3567.

Library of Congress Cataloging-in-Publication Data

Bryan, Nichol, 1958-
    Chernobyl: nuclear disaster / by Nichol Bryan.
      p. cm. — (Environmental disasters)
    Summary: Discusses the disastrous 1986 accident at the Chernobyl nuclear power plant in the Ukraine.
Includes bibliographical references and index.
    ISBN 0-8368-5504-3 (lib. bdg.)
    ISBN 0-8368-5511-6 (softcover)
    1. Chernobyl Nuclear Accident, Chornobyl§' Ukraine, 1986—Juvenile literature. 2. Disasters—
Environmental aspects—Juvenile literature. 3. Nuclear power plants—Ukraine—Chernobyl—Accidents—
Juvenile literature. [1. Chernobyl Nuclear Accident, Chornobyl§' Ukraine, 1986. 2. Nuclear power plants—
Accidents.] I. Title. II. Series.
    TK1362.U38B79   2003
    363.17'99'094776—dc21   2003042291

First published in 2004 by
World Almanac® Library
330 West Olive Street, Suite 100
Milwaukee, WI 53212 USA

Copyright © 2004 by World Almanac® Library.

Produced by Lownik Communication Services
Cover design and page production: Heidi Bittner-Zastrow
Picture researcher: Jean Lownik
World Almanac® Library art direction: Tammy Gruenewald
World Almanac® Library series editor: Carol Ryback

Photo Credits: Cover, 26, 27, AFP PHOTO/EPA/VICTOR DRACHEV © AFP/CORBIS; 4, Heidi Bittner-Zastrow; 5, 31,
© AFP/CORBIS; © CORBIS; 7, 9, 12, 23, 25, © GREENPEACE / CLIVE SHIRLEY; 8, © Peter Turnley/CORBIS; 10,
22, 42, © Yann Arthus-Bertrand/CORBIS; 11, 34, 36(r), AFP PHOTO/EPA/SERGEI SUPINSKY © AFP/CORBIS; 13,
© Bettmann/CORBIS; 14, Thomas Szlukovenyi © Reuters NewMedia Inc./CORBIS; 15, Soviet Archives; 16, Courtesy
Nuclear Energy Institute; 17, © Ed Eckstein/CORBIS; 18, 19, 20, 21, © KOSTIN IGOR/CORBIS SYGMA; 24, Wally
McNamee/CORBIS; 28, Courtesy National Atmospheric Release Advisory Center; 29, © Reuters; 30, 33, © Caroline
Penn/CORBIS; 36(l), Reuters/Gleb Garanich © Reuters NewMedia Inc./CORBIS; 37, © Brian A. Vikander/CORBIS;
38(b), AFP PHOTO/EPA © AFP/CORBIS; 38(t), AFP PHOTO/EPA/POOL/Konstantin Diordiev © AFP/CORBIS; 41,
Courtesy U.S. Department of Energy, Energy Information Administration; 43, © GREENPEACE / ALEXANDER SHIGAEV

Printed in the United States of America

1 2 3 4 5 6 7 8 9 07 06 05 04 03

Cover: Solnechny, Belarus, was evacuated after the 1986 Chernobyl disaster.
Solnechny is in the 19-mile (30-kilometer) radius Exclusion Zone near
the Ukrainian nuclear power plant. "Solnechny" means "sunny."

Contents

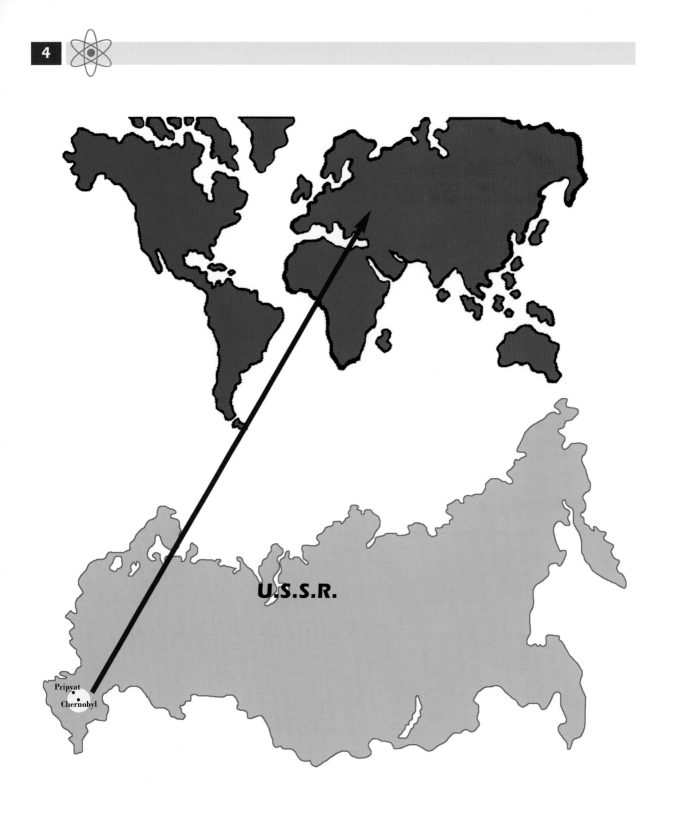

U.S.S.R.

Pripyat

Chernobyl

 Introduction

Nuclear Energy Out of Control

The nuclear power plant at Chernobyl, Ukraine, exploded with an earth-shaking roar. For most victims, however, death came silently.

While some plant workers and fire fighters died in the initial explosion or while fighting the fires that followed, most of those who suffered and died did so quietly. They were victims of a silent killer — radiation. Many died months or years later from cancer caused by the exposure to radiation. Even today, some are fighting illnesses related to the terrific explosion.

The Chernobyl nuclear accident on April 26, 1986, was the world's worst nuclear accident ever, and a global catastrophe. It was global because the

French scientists, wearing protective suits and gas masks, measure the radioactivity on a farm about 4 miles (6 kilometers) from the Chernobyl nuclear power plant in 1999.

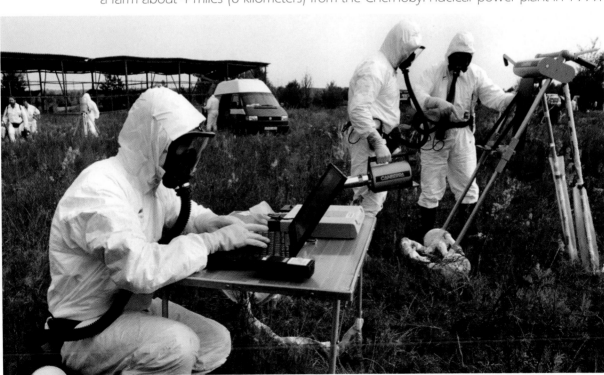

radioactive plumes of smoke drifted across several nations. Fallout traveled across Ukraine, in the former Soviet Union, where the plant was located, into the neighboring Soviet state of Belarus. It dropped radioactive isotopes — such as cesium 137 and strontium 90 — on crops, animals, and people as it moved.

The radioactive plume was not limited to the Soviet Union. It drifted across northern Europe and kept going. On the opposite side of the planet, radiation detectors in Canada and the United States measured fallout from Chernobyl. Only the Southern Hemisphere remained free of contamination.

A Global Catastrophe

Chernobyl was a global catastrophe for other reasons as well. It affected worldwide opinions about nuclear power. The "No Nukes" movement against nuclear energy gained momentum as protesters swelled in numbers. Governments felt more pressure to cancel nuclear power plants planned for construction and to shut down older plants long before they were scheduled to close. Around the world, countries began to look for alternatives to nuclear power. Many turned to coal-fired power plants — which present their own environmental problems, such as acid rain. In the United States, political and social pressures increased regarding the development of domestic

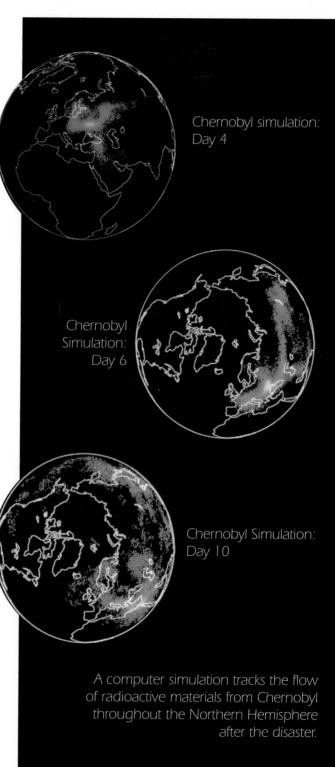

Chernobyl simulation: Day 4

Chernobyl Simulation: Day 6

Chernobyl Simulation: Day 10

A computer simulation tracks the flow of radioactive materials from Chernobyl throughout the Northern Hemisphere after the disaster.

sources of energy, such as offshore oil drilling or drilling in environmentally sensitive areas in Alaska.

Whatever alternatives the industrialized countries pursued, one thing was sure. The dream of plentiful, inexpensive, clean electrical power from nuclear power was over. The vision of energy that would transform the world — energy that would be "too cheap to meter" — was dead. In a real sense, it died in Chernobyl.

The Chernobyl disaster had other far-reaching effects. The Soviet government kept news of the accident quiet — as was its practice for other natural and man-made disasters in the past. But as radiation levels began to soar in countries such as Finland and Sweden, the Soviet Union's communist leaders had to admit something had gone terribly wrong and appealed to the world for help.

For the Soviets, Chernobyl was an embarrassment of international proportions. It was a sign to the whole world — and to Soviet citizens themselves — that the communist government was inept and deceitful. At a time when it

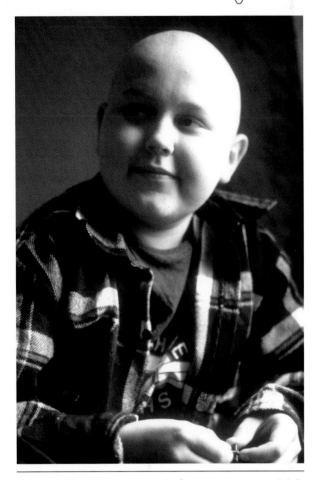

Chemotherapy treatments for cancer caused this child to lose his hair. Cancer is a disease that often causes cells to mutate, divide very rapidly, and spread throughout the body. People living near Chernobyl who were exposed to very high radiation doses may still develop cancer after all these years — but even small amounts of radiation may cause cancer.

"**Chernobyl . . .** had a significant impact on human society. Not only did it produce severe health consequences and physical, industrial and economic damage in the short term, but, also, its long-term consequences in terms of socio-economic disruption, psychological stress and damaged image of nuclear energy, are expected to be long standing."

— European Nuclear Energy Agency

"Good evening, comrades. All of you know that there has been an incredible misfortune — the accident at the Chernobyl nuclear plant. It has painfully affected the Soviet people, and shocked the international community. For the first time, we confront the real force of nuclear energy, out of control."

— Soviet President Mikhail Gorbachev, announcing the accident on state television

touted its nuclear power program as a sign of the modernism and economic strength of the communist system, the disaster made the Soviet rulers look powerless. The slow response and haphazard nature of its evacuation and preventive treatment program generated angry frustration at home and criticism from abroad.

Many historians credit the Chernobyl accident as one of the events that delivered the final blow to the Soviet Union's credibility. In a way, it was the beginning of the end of the Soviet system itself. Within four years of the accident, the Soviet Union had fallen. Its member states split up into fifteen separate countries. Communism itself began to retreat. Most of the countries of Eastern Europe adopted Western-style democratic capitalist systems. Even Asian communist states like China and Vietnam became more open to capitalist ways of life.

Today, the Soviet Union is nothing but a memory. But the deadly legacy of Chernobyl continues. Throughout the region, levels of radioactive elements remain very high. Negative health effects — cancer, birth defects, diseases, and other medical conditions — caused by the radiation continues to claim lives. Produce, meat, and dairy products from the region are monitored for radioactivity. Two decades later, much of this food is discarded.

The lives of the people of the Chernobyl region are forever changed.

The Sarcophagus (Greek for "stone coffin") encases about 200 tons (181 tonnes) of radioactive fuel, fuel dust, and chunks of Unit 4's melted reactor core. The hastily built concrete-and-metal structure is deteriorating. Engineers say that safety inspections of its roof and sides revealed at least 1,200 square yards (1,000 square meters) of holes and leaks. These openings allow snow and rainwater to seep in, causing further breakdown of the building. Birds and other animals also enter and leave through these holes, spreading radioactive dust. A special 20,000-ton (18,100-tonne) weatherproof shell 370 feet (113 m) high is being constructed off-site and will be rolled into place over the Sarcophagus in 2007. Although the new covering should last about 100 years, it is not designed to contain the radioactivity still being emitted.

The economy continues to suffer. Rates of depression and suicide remain high. The wreckage at Chernobyl will remain dangerous for centuries.

A hulking, vault-like building that covers the ruins of the Unit 4 reactor dominates the landscape. Its vault has lived up to its name — the Sarcophagus — which means "stone coffin."

It truly is a chamber of death.

 Chapter 1

The Peaceful Atom

People felt lucky to live in Pripyat, Ukraine. The town is located about 80 miles (129 kilometers) from Kiev, the capital of Ukraine. Today, Ukraine is an independent nation. But in the 1980s, it was one of the states of the Union of Soviet Socialist Republics (U.S.S.R.), also called the Soviet Union. Back then, Ukraine was ruled by the communist Soviet government. The Soviets wanted Pripyat to serve as an example of everything good and wonderful that the communist economic and political system could achieve.

High radiation levels from the Chernobyl accident caused the evacuation and abandonment of entire cities, such as Pripyat. The quarantined area, or "Exclusion Zone," came to be known simply as "The Zone."

Brown's Ferry Accident

A fire at the Browns Ferry nuclear plant in Athens, Alabama, almost caused a meltdown in 1975. Two electricians were looking for air leaks in a room where most of the electrical cables for the plant ran through. They were using lit candles to check for the leaks because the air would cause the candle flame to flicker. The candles set fire to some rubber foam. The fire burned through the cables controlling many of the safety features of the plant, including its emergency cooling system. It also knocked out many of the instruments that told operators what was happening in the reactor. Workers finally were able to shut the reactor down after the fire was put out, hours later.

Pripyat's clean and modern apartment buildings lined the wide and well-kept streets. Food was fairly plentiful, even though it was often in short supply in other parts of the Soviet Union. The young, well-educated citizens of Pripyat were mostly there for one purpose — to serve the massive nuclear generating plant just 10 miles (16 km) away, at Chernobyl.

The Chernobyl plant was one of the largest power producers in the Soviet Union. But it stood for more than that. For the government, Chernobyl was a sign to the rest of the world of how science and technology served the needs of the Soviet people. White-coated plant workers walked to their jobs under a sign that said, "Make peace stronger by your labor!"

"I wasn't afraid to take a job at a nuclear power plant," a young turbine operator said in a magazine article

Workers forego protective gear in March 1999 as they scrub dirt and radioactive dust from the floor of the Chernobyl nuclear power plant in preparation to restart the plant's third power block.

published in early 1986. "There is more emotion in [the] fear of nuclear power plants than real danger. I work in white overalls. The air is clean and fresh." Government energy officials pointed with pride to Chernobyl's safe design. The odds of a meltdown, they said, were 1 in 10,000 years.

Nuclear Dreams

The Soviets were not alone in their enthusiasm for nuclear power. In the 1950s and 1960s, the promise of atomic energy excited many. The first nuclear weapons, which helped end World War II, showed the world the incredible power gained from splitting the atom. Scientists hoped to harness this energy to produce electricity. They believed that nuclear power plants would usher in a new era of cheap energy.

"A Dream of a Town"
"Pripyat . . . was a dream of a town, built by the young and for the young: the average age [in] the 48,000-[person] town was twenty-six years. It was one of the best-provided towns in the Soviet Union. The best merchandise was brought there; the most popular artists came to perform there. Lots of flowers and birds, lots of smiles and happy laughter. The air was filled with the expectation of happiness and love."
— Alla Feofanofa, Ukrainian journalist

Radiation ruined the harvest within the radius in a 19-mile (30-km) Exclusion Zone around Chernobyl. All crops must be destroyed. Experts predict that food from The Zone will remain unsafe for about three hundred years.

There were many reasons to be excited by nuclear power. Although radioactive fuels like uranium were hard to find, small quantities could produce incredible amounts of energy. Just over 2 pounds (1 kilogram) of uranium can produce almost 19 million kilowatt-hours of energy — enough to power entire cities. Compared to the thousands of tons of coal and millions of barrels of oil that Western nations needed to burn to produce electricity, uranium appeared to be the ideal fuel of the future.

Nuclear power had another benefit over other energy sources. The fission process produces no smoke, no ash, no soot. Coal, on the other hand, gives off black, acrid smoke and poison gases when burned. Major industrial cities that burned huge amounts of coal for heat and electricity turned dirty and grimy. People around the world were becoming aware of the dangers of the air pollution coal created. In London, England, the combination of weather patterns and air pollution from burning coal often produced smoggy days that residents called "pea soupers" because the air seemed to be as thick as pea soup. Thousands of people died from lung diseases during the London "pea souper" of 1952. By contrast, nuclear power seemed spotlessly clean.

The promise of nuclear power gave rise to bright predictions of a revolution in human society. Some of the most enthusiastic supporters of nuclear

The dangers of radiation were not fully known when nuclear power and weapons were first developed. This 1951 photo shows U.S. troops observing a nuclear bomb's poisonous mushroom cloud during a training exercise.

"Too Cheap to Meter"

"It is not too much to expect that our children will enjoy in their homes electricity too cheap to meter, will know of great periodic regional famines in the world only as matters of history, will travel effortlessly over the seas and under them and through the air with a minimum of danger at great speeds, and will experience a life span far longer than ours as disease yields and man comes to understand what causes him to age."

— Lewis L. Strauss, Chairman of the U.S. Atomic Energy Commission, in a 1954 speech on nuclear energy

power thought that it would be so plentiful and cheap that it would cost users almost nothing. With so much free power, humans could solve the problems of poverty and hunger. Writers imagined nuclear-powered airplanes that would let commuters travel faster than sound and nuclear spaceships that would propel us to other planets and beyond. "No baseball game will be called off on account of rain in the Era of Atomic Energy," predicted science writer David Dietz in 1945. "No airplane will bypass an airport because of fog. No city will experience a winter traffic jam because of snow. Summer resorts will be able to guarantee the weather and artificial suns will make it as easy to grow corn and potatoes indoors as on a farm."

No wonder so many countries invested heavily in nuclear power — the United States alone built more than one hundred plants between 1944 and 1985. The amount of U.S. electricity provided

Some three thousand wooden crosses were placed near the nuclear power plant in Bohunice, Czechoslovakia, to commemorate the Chernobyl nuclear disaster five years earlier.

by nuclear power grew to 20 percent. In countries such as France, with fewer coal supplies, almost three-quarters of all electricity was generated by nuclear power plants by the mid-1980s.

Growing Concerns

But as the worldwide nuclear industry grew, so did the concerns about its safety. Science began to learn more about the effects of nuclear radiation on the human body. In the early days of the atomic bomb, scientists felt that most of the danger from nuclear power came from the massive amounts of radioactive fallout produced by a nuclear explosion. As medical researchers dug deeper, they learned that radiation caused cancer in much smaller doses than first thought.

Also, a series of accidents at nuclear plants with names like Browns Ferry and Three Mile Island showed that nuclear plants were far from foolproof. People became concerned about how to dispose of the used atomic fuel rods, which remained dangerously radioactive for thousands of years. Plutonium, one of the elements in these "spent" fuel rods, is also one of the most deadly substances known. And, plutonium can be used to make atomic bombs. Many worried that the spread of nuclear power plants could lead to more countries having nuclear weapons.

Top-secret KGB documents discovered after the Chernobyl nuclear disaster warned of safety problems at the plant.

Some people in the United States and Europe began to call for an end to nuclear power. They pressured governments to increase the safety regulations for nuclear power plants. The growing popular fear of nuclear power led many power companies to drop plans for building new plants, although they continued to use the nuclear plants already built.

But in the Soviet Union, warnings about the dangers of nuclear power were kept hushed. For the Soviets, developing

How Nuclear Power Plants Work

Nuclear power plants produce energy through a process called nuclear fission. Fission is the breaking apart of an atom's center, or nucleus. It happens because some elements, called radioactive elements, are unstable — which means they naturally lose, or "shoot out," neutrons from their nucleus. These neutrons hit the centers of other atoms, causing them to split as well. When the atoms split, they release energy in the form of heat. They also shoot out more neutrons, which hit the centers of even more atoms in a chain reaction.

All nuclear power plants work in about the same way. Radioactive uranium fuel rods are placed just close enough together in a pool of water so that their neutrons can strike each other. As the atoms split apart, the rods heat up, heating the water around them. The water turns to steam, and the energy from the steam powers turbines — which spin to create electricity. The chain reaction can be slowed down by lowering graphite control rods between the fuel rods. Graphite soaks up some of the loose neutrons, which cools the radioactive reactor water.

In most Western-built reactors, the reactor water doesn't touch the turbines. Instead, this radioactive water transfers heat to a separate, closed loop of fresh, non-radioactive water. The steam in the second loop turns the turbines. This two-loop system prevent the escape of radioactive steam. Chernobyl had only one loop and used radioactive steam to power its turbines.

Only two things — the control rods and the water — keep the fuel rods from getting too hot and melting down. If there is a problem with the control rods, or if there's not enough water in the reactor, an accident can happen.

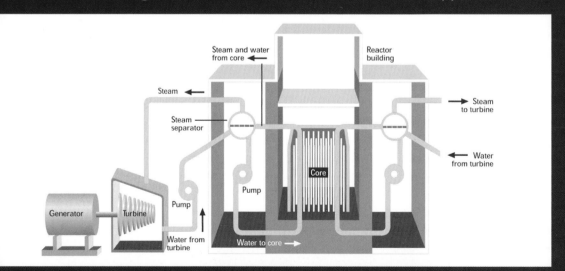

This diagram of a nuclear reactor is similar to the design of the Chernobyl nuclear power plant.

a strong nuclear power program went hand-in-hand with building an arsenal of nuclear missiles. It was a way to show Western nations — and especially the U.S. — that the Soviets would not fall behind in the race for new technology. Because the U.S.S.R.'s nuclear program was a source of national pride, the communist government often arrested anyone who criticized it.

Soviet planners cut many corners in their rush to develop nuclear energy. They compromised on safety because they felt sure nothing could go wrong. Officials told the public that there was nuclear power plants were completely safe. Behind closed doors in the Soviet capital of Moscow, however, government officials had some concerns.

The four separate nuclear reactors at Chernobyl were designed very differently from the ones in the United States. There were no concrete and steel structures around the reactors to prevent the release of radiation in case of an accident. The Soviet plants were designed so that there was enough water to cool the fuel rods

An anti-nuke protester stands under a marquee advertising the 1979 movie, *The China Syndrome*. The movie is about a reporter who witnesses an accident at a nuclear power plant.

and slow the fission process when the reactor was in full operation. But if power dropped, there was a danger that too much of the water would turn to steam. Without flowing water, the fuel rods would heat up and the fission in the reactor core might get out of control.

In fact, as early as 1979, a top-secret Soviet report noted, "According to data in the possession of the KGB of the Soviet Union, design deviations and violations of construction and assembly technology are occurring at various places in the construction of the second generating unit of the Chernobyl [nuclear power plant] and these could lead to mishaps and accidents." The government never shared this dire warning with the Soviet people.

"The China Syndrome"

No matter where in the world it occurs, the worst nuclear accident experts can imagine is nicknamed the "China Syndrome." In a China Syndrome scenario, runaway heat in a reactor causes a "meltdown," which means all the fuel rods melt together. This super-hot molten fuel blob then burns its way through the floor of the containment vessel and into the ground itself — supposedly all the way from North America through the planet to China. Actually, experts think the fuel would burn down until it hit groundwater, when it would release an explosion of radioactive steam. So far, no nuclear accident has ever turned into a China Syndrome event.

Chapter 2

"The Invisible Monster"

April 25, 1986, was supposed to be a routine day at the Chernobyl nuclear plant. One of the reactors, Unit 4, was scheduled to be shut down for normal maintenance. A team of technicians decided to take advantage of the shutdown to do a safety test of the reactor. They wanted to find out if

A victim of the Chernobyl nuclear accident is wrapped in protective bandages.

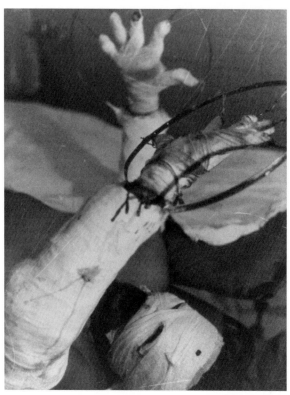

the plant's turbines would provide enough power to keep the reactor cool if there was a general power outage.

Plant workers planned to slow the turbines that generated the plant's power and monitor the water as it flowed through the reactor core. To discover how the plant responded all by itself, its emergency backup cooling system would be turned off. Plant staff had run these kinds of tests before, but they needed more information to tell for sure if the plant was safe in a low-power situation.

That evening, technicians began to slow the plant's turbines. At first, the power output dropped normally. But just after midnight, the power from the turbine fell faster than expected. As the water flow in the reactor slowed, more and more steam built up. The more the steam built up, the faster the fission reaction in the core increased. To make matters worse, the testers were not using enough control rods in the reactor to slow down the fission process. Worried, they dropped all the plant's control rods into the reactor by hand. By 1:00 A.M. on April 26, the power was finally under control.

But the testers had created a situation that brought out the worst in the Chernobyl plant's design. Because the same water that cooled the reactor also ran the turbines, the process that controlled the reactor started to seesaw. As the turbines turned faster, the water flowed more quickly in the reactor and cooled it down. Consequently, as the heat in the reactor dropped, it produced less steam to power the turbines, so the turbine slowed down. Plant operators made constant adjustments to the speed of the turbines and the placement of the fuel rods in a frantic attempt to control the reactor.

This bird's-eye view of Chernobyl's destroyed Reactor 4 was taken from the top of Reactor 3. High levels of radiation lingered in the area and deteriorated the quality of the film, which affected the clarity of the photograph.

Chernobyl Explodes

At 1:23 A.M., the operators at Chernobyl lost the battle. Power output in the reactor suddenly jumped to one hundred times the normal amount. The radioactive fuel in the reactor core started to burst apart. The steam in the reactor core exploded. Seconds later, another explosion ripped through the reactor. The twin explosions destroyed the core of Unit 4 and blew off the reactor's 1,100-ton (1,000-tonne) roof.

The explosions sent a geyser of radioactive material almost 1 mile (1.6 km) into the air. With the super-hot core exposed to oxygen, the reactor debris burst into flames. A thick, black plume of radioactive smoke billowed up, drifting downwind. Scientists later estimated that the amount of radioactivity released by the explosion and the fires was two hundred times greater than the radiation from the U.S. atomic bombs dropped in Japan on Hiroshima and Nagasaki at the end of World War II.

The heat caused over thirty fires to erupt all around the plant. More than one hundred firefighters rushed from Pripyat to put out the blazes. The fire fighters had no special clothing to protect them from the radiation streaming from the wreckage. Many did not even know the danger they faced.

By late afternoon, many of the smaller fires around the plant had been put out. Then a new blaze erupted. The

Although he is carrying equipment that measures the radioactivity levels of Chernobyl, this technician has removed his mask. The photo illustrates what critics called a lack of a safety culture at the plant.

"A Lack of Safety Culture"

"In summary, the Chernobyl accident was the product of a lack of 'safety culture.' The reactor design was poor from the point of view of safety and unforgiving for the operators, both of which provoked a dangerous operating state. The operators were not informed of this and were not aware that the test performed could have brought the reactor into explosive conditions. In addition, they did not comply with established operational procedures. The combination of these factors provoked a nuclear accident of maximum severity in which the reactor was totally destroyed within a few seconds."

— From a European Atomic Energy Commission report

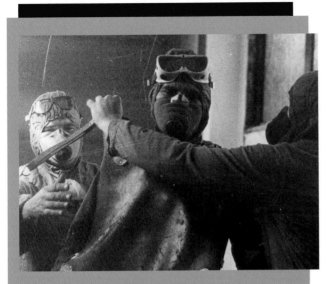

An Alarm in the Night

"My husband was woken by an alarm on the night of 26 April 1986. He came home the next evening. He was one of the drivers for the military motorcade which responded to the accident when the alarm was first raised. Both trucks and drivers had to wait for some time in the 'auburn forest,' but their dosimeters were broken so no one knew what radiation doses they had received. During the rest of that year, Volodymyr went to 'The Zone' several times and his total working period was 152 hours. In 1987, he suddenly lost his consciousness while driving the car and caused an accident. But Volodymyr was an experienced driver who had been worked for a long time in the north without any such problems. I don't think it was coincidence."

— Vika Troschuk, whose husband, Volodymyr, transported soldiers to and from dangerous sites during the Chernobyl cleanup.

Before the concrete Sarcophagus was built, teams were sent to clean the roof of Reactor Unit 3. Radiation was so high that each outing was limited to forty seconds.

graphite used in the reactor core began to burn. Graphite is a form of carbon, similar to coal. It burns with an intense heat. Firefighters couldn't put out the graphite fire with water. It burned for ten days, sending more radioactive smoke into the air.

More than thirty people were killed at Chernobyl. Most of them were plant workers killed in the explosion and firefighters who died putting out the blazes that followed. But 137 more would die in the following weeks because of the radiation they absorbed while fighting the fire. Many of these victims became so radioactive that doctors and nurses were afraid to help them.

The danger was not limited to Chernobyl, however. The smoke plumes from the plant drifted through the atmosphere, dropping radioactive particles along the way. Soon, hundreds of thousands of people living around the plant were exposed to high doses of lethal radiation.

A Silent Killer

Radiation causes most of its damage by attacking DNA. DNA is the material in almost every body cell that tells it how to divide and reproduce. You can think of it as a code for building the body. The code in DNA is made up of a string of

A View from the Air

"The next day we took a helicopter and flew around the site. We saw pieces of graphite lying around on fire, and the damaged block that looked like . . . well, Hell. Witnessing a nuclear reactor on fire is terrible, especially for a physicist."

— Former Soviet nuclear specialist Nikolai Smirnov

Chernobyl spawned many radioactive junkyards. Helicopters, cranes, and other equipment became so contaminated during the cleanup that it was abandoned.

chemicals. These chemicals must link in just the right sequence, or code, to produce healthy new cells that do their job normally.

Radiation exposure can change the code of the DNA. This change is called a mutation. Sometimes mutated cells just die. But mutated cells can also start to divide very fast and out of control. This wild cell division is what causes cancer. Even small amounts of radiation can cause cancer in this way.

Thyroid cancer is a common cancer that develops from radiation exposure. The thyroid is a gland in the neck that uses iodine to control how the body grows and how fast it produces energy from food. When a person is exposed to radioactive iodine from nuclear fallout, most of it winds up in the thyroid gland.

Radiation can also cause mutations in the sperm cells in men and the egg cells in women. This changes the DNA code that tells the cells how to make a healthy baby. When this happens, or when a mother who is expecting a baby is exposed to radiation, the child can die before it is born. It can also be born with serious physical problems.

All of the residents downwind of Chernobyl now faced these risks. And none of them knew what was coming.

"It Was Forbidden to Talk About This."

"It is so strange and scary to watch the films of that time . . . featuring soldiers dressed in radiation protective overalls tightly done up with respirators and gas masks walking like aliens from outer space among the civilians: children playing in the playgrounds, women carrying their shopping bags, wedding processions going along the streets.

"It was hot: People were wearing light summer clothes with uncovered arms and legs exposed to the radiation. Nobody had instructed them what to do in the case of such an accident. It was strictly forbidden to talk about this. 'Your husbands got poisoned with gases,' the families of the firefighters were told."

— Story told by Ludmila, wife of Chernobyl firefighter

A gas mask lies in the hallway of an abandoned secondary school near Chernobyl.

Chapter 3

The Global Alarm

It would take firefighters at Chernobyl almost two weeks to stop the graphite fire that was belching radioactive smoke into the air. Nobody in the Soviet Union knew how to fight such a fire. In fact, very few people anywhere in the world knew anything about graphite fires.

Firefighters decided to rob the fire of oxygen by dropping materials on it. Using giant helicopters, workers dropped 5,500 tons (5,000 tonnes) of lead, boron, sand, and clay onto the reactor. They hoped the lead and boron particles would absorb radiation as the sand and clay smothered the flames.

Three Mile Island Accident

The 1979 accident at the Three Mile Island nuclear plant in Pennsylvania was not as serious as the accident at Chernobyl. Operators at the plant accidentally shut off safety systems at the plant during an emergency shutdown. The loss of coolant damaged the reactor core, which released a small amount of radioactive gas into the air. Although the accident posed little health risk, it caused widespread alarm. In response, Congress passed new laws calling for tougher regulation of nuclear power plants. Three Mile Island was the worst U.S. nuclear accident, and it changed many people's minds about the safety of nuclear power.

On March 28, 1979, one of the reactor cores at Three Mile Island nuclear power plant near Middletown, Pennsylvania, experienced a partial meltdown after a series of equipment failures complicated by human errors. Although the plant's cooling towers became the symbol for the accident, they were not the site of the radioactive steam release. The release was the most serious U.S. nuclear accident, but most of the damage and radioactivity was contained.

Firefighters inside "The Zone" at Chernobyl did not use any special equipment for working in radioactive areas.

Trying to hit the reactor in the dense smoke turned out to be a hard task. Much of the material missed the target. Worse, the helicopter pilots died quickly from the massive amount of radiation they received. The helicopters and other fire-fighting equipment often became so radioactive that they were abandoned.

By May 9, twelve days after the accident, the graphite fire burned itself out. But the plant remained extremely dangerous. Officials worried that the nuclear material in the ruined core might start heating up again.

They were afraid the nuclear fuel might burn into the ground and hit the groundwater — causing a "China Syndrome" catastrophe.

Emergency workers at the site began building a huge concrete slab under the damaged reactor. About four hundred workers tunneled under the plant and built the slab, which had a built-in cooling system to keep the reactor core from overheating.

Thousands of people involved in putting out the fires, building the containment slab, and cleaning up

Almost two-thirds of the cancer patients at this medical center in Belarus come from areas poisoned by radioactive dust from Chernobyl.

radioactive waste at the site were e xposed to massive amounts of radiation. About half of them were soldiers who had no choice but to obey orders. They were hailed as heroes by the Soviet government, but they soon developed health problems. The government came up with a special name for these workers at Chernobyl: liquidators.

A Slow Evacuation

Soviet officials were slow to tell people who lived in the area about the danger. They did not want to create a panic. They also hoped to avoid sharing the news of this huge failure of the Soviet nuclear program.

Officials held off evacuating Pripyat until it became clear that radiation was reaching high levels. On the morning of April 27, a day after the accident, residents of the town were told to leave. But the refugees had already absorbed high doses of radiation.

"I Saw This With My Own Eyes."
"Let me outline my own experiences of the Chernobyl accident. My family — I have two children — were in Kiev at that time. We had to keep them indoors with all the windows tightly sealed for days. And I am uncertain as to whether they received dangerous doses of radiation. We drove to Dnepropetrovsk on May 8 and were stopped at one of the police stations there because they noticed that our car had Kiev license plants. They had a man on duty with a geiger counter that measured simply gamma rays. He put the geiger counter to the thyroid glands of both children and the reading was much higher than for any other part of the body. I saw this with my own eyes."

— Yuri Risovanny,
Pripyat Industrial and Research Association

After more stalling, officials realized that a much larger area around the Chernobyl plant was being dangerously contaminated by fallout from the fires. They decided to evacuate everybody within a 19-mile (30-km) radius of the plant. This circle became known as the Exclusion Zone, or just "The Zone." In total, about 135,000 people living in The Zone were forced to leave their homes. Most would never be allowed to return.

Even as it was evacuating thousands of people, the Soviet government kept the accident a secret — from its own people and from the world. But wind patterns carried the radioactive plume away from the plant, northwest across Belarus, Poland, and Sweden.

Mysterious Radiation

On April 28, Cliff Robinson, an engineer at Forsmark Nuclear Plant 50 miles (80 km) northeast of Uppsala, Sweden, walked through a radiation detector to get to his office. He was startled to hear the detector alarm go

An elderly Belarussian couple, carrying their remaining belongings, trudge past a dwelling that is being destroyed as part of a total radiation cleaning in their village.

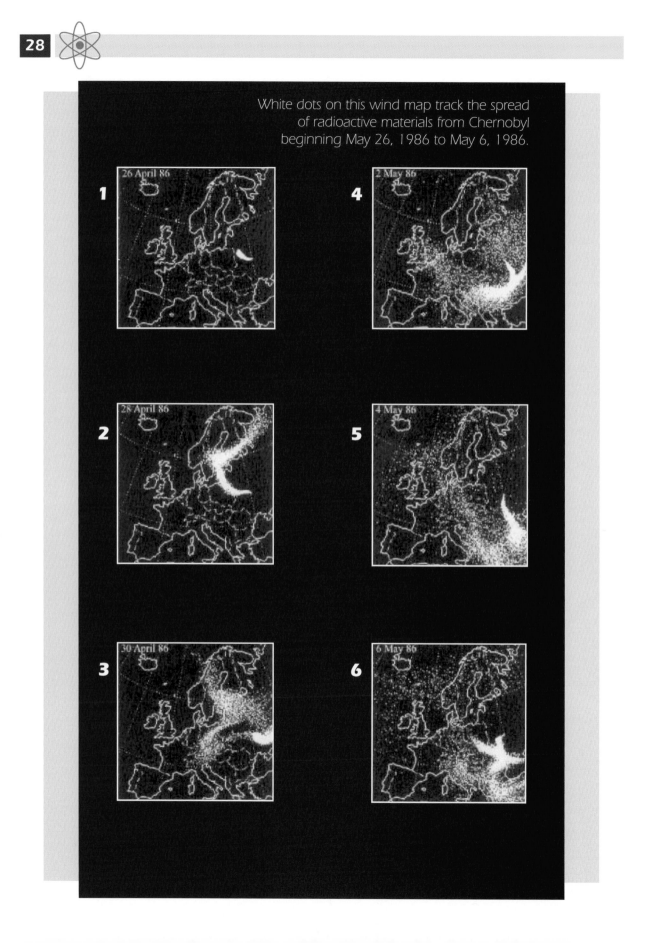

White dots on this wind map track the spread of radioactive materials from Chernobyl beginning May 26, 1986 to May 6, 1986.

A youngster swallows an anti-radiation iodine solution in a Warsaw clinic on April 30, 1986, shortly after the Chernobyl disaster.

off. When Robinson measured the radioactivity of his shoes, he found levels never seen around the plant before. "My first thought was that a war had broken out and that somebody had blown up a nuclear bomb," Robinson recalled.

At first, Swedish officials thought the radiation might be coming from the Forsmark plant itself. But they soon learned that the radioactive dust was being carried by the wind — from the direction of the Soviet Union. European diplomats asked officials in Moscow what was happening. They got no answer. But quietly, the Soviet government asked Sweden, West Germany, and Britain for advice on how to put out a graphite fire. On April 28, with concern rising around the world, the Soviet people were only told in a short statement on government-run Moscow TV that "an accident had occurred at the Chernobyl nuclear power plant." The story gave no details.

The next morning, intelligence agents in the United States looked at a photo of the Chernobyl plant taken by a high-power spy satellite. They were shocked to see the roof blown completely off the

Struggling with the Invisible Monster

"The night of the explosion I was on duty with the Chernobyl nuclear power plant guard platoon. I can still remember how people struggled with the invisible monster that had been let loose. My family was evacuated from Pripyat, but we remained on duty until we were replaced.

"I begun to have health problems in the first few years, but I attributed them to the first hard months of adapting to a new environment, to family problems, to problems of employment and residence, and other causes. But over the past three years it has become worse although I do not smoke or drink excessive alcohol. Both my wife and myself are now certified as Level 3 disabled persons. My children (my son aged sixteen and my daughter aged nine) also have some health problems associated with the consequences of the Chernobyl disaster. We are a typical Pripyat family of liquidators."

— Vasiliy Osipovich Kotetsky, a guard on duty
at the Chernobyl plant the night of the accident.

Valentina Rogova shows her 1995 identification from her days as a liquidator at Chernobyl.

reactor, with smoke billowing into the air. The photo also showed that the nearby town of Pripyat had still not been completely evacuated. The U.S. released the photo as evidence the Soviets were not telling the truth about Chernobyl.

It wasn't until April 30, four days after the accident, that the Moscow newspaper *Pravda* began to release information about the accident. The government-run media showed the U.S. satellite photo of the plant — but with the smoke from the ruins carefully removed from the image.

Across the world, people responded to the news of the accident with fear — and sometimes panic. Because the

Farmer Andrey Rudchenko drinks fresh milk from one of his cows in the highly radioactive zone around the devastated Chernobyl nuclear reactor. About two hundred people have returned to The Zone, even though it is a forbidden area.

Soviets were being so secretive, no one was sure how bad the accident was or where the radiation might spread. They were afraid of being exposed to radioactive dust falling from the air. But they were also afraid of radioactive elements finding their way into drinking water, food, and milk.

Poland immediately distributed iodine tablets to children to keep their thyroid glands from absorbing radioactive iodine from Chernobyl's fallout. Thyroid cancer is often one of the first cancers that come from radiation exposure.

West Germany, Austria, and Britain placed restrictions on farmers selling meat, milk, and crops in areas that were

President Reagan Responds

"We are comforted by Mr. Gorbachev's assurances that 'the worst is behind us' in dealing with the Chernobyl reactor tragedy. . . . We are distressed, however, that Mr. Gorbachev used the occasion of his otherwise reassuring presentation to make unfounded charges against the United States and other Western governments. . . . The United States Government at no point encouraged inaccurate reporting on the accident. If some reports carried in the mass media were in fact inaccurate, this was an inevitable result of the extreme secrecy with which the Soviet authorities dealt with the accident in the days immediately following it."

— Statement by Larry Speakes,
President Ronald Reagan's press secretary, May 14, 1986

contaminated with radiation. Many countries destroyed food that they believed was contaminated. Even on the other side of the world, in Canada, people were warned not to drink rainwater and to have their wells tested for radioactivity.

People also became alarmed about nuclear power plants operating around the globe. They were afraid that the plants in their own countries might explode the way Chernobyl did. Officials tried to calm people by explaining that few countries outside the Soviet Union had Chernobyl-style plants. But people were still afraid.

Nations throughout the world offered to help the Soviets fight the fires at Chernobyl and clean up the site. They wanted to make sure the disaster didn't get any worse. But the Soviet government was slow to accept offers of help. Soviet leader Mikhail Gorbachev accused Western countries of trying to make the Soviet Union look bad.

Chapter 4

In the Shadow of Chernobyl

In the months that followed the Chernobyl accident, the Soviet government struggled to cope with the consequences. Military barricades kept people out of the Exclusion Zone surrounding the plant. Outside the zone, soldiers worked to reduce the radiation exposure people faced. They washed down the outside of buildings, especially schools, hospitals, and other public buildings.

Paved streets were also washed down, and dirt roads were kept watered so that radioactive dust wouldn't rise into the air. People in the area were given iodine pills to try to protect them from thyroid cancer. Tons of radioactive topsoil were scooped up and hauled away to special storage sites.

A warning sign marks this radioactive forest near Chernobyl, Ukraine.

Over five hundred scientists and specialists from around the world gathered in Kiev to mark Chernobyl's fifteenth anniversary. These scientists are measuring radiation levels near the Sarcophagus.

Building the Sarcophagus

Meanwhile, at the Chernobyl plant, workers tried to stop any new radiation leaks from the ruins of Unit 4. Scientists feared that the nuclear fuel still in the reactor core might melt down uncontrollably. To head off another disaster, workers used 392,385 cubic yards (300,000 cubic meters) of cement to construct enormous concrete walls all around the damaged reactor. They topped it off with a 6,600-ton (6,000-tonne) steel roof. The structure was finished in November, just seven months after the accident. Some people referred to the huge containment building as "the envelope." But the more popular name for it was the Sarcophagus.

As massive as the Sarcophagus was, it was never meant to last. Authorities just

Chernobyl and the Fall of the Soviet Union

"Chernobyl was also probably the catalyst and major factor in awakening the captive nations in the U.S.S.R. to struggle for their independence. The citizens of Ukraine finally realized that Moscow was destroying their environment and endangering the health and lives of all the people. This was the inspiration for the Rukh movement which spearheaded the nation to seek freedom from Moscow. The long struggle ended with the demise of the U.S.S.R. and the independence of Ukraine on August 24, 1991."

— Ukrainian Historian Andrew Gregorovich

wanted to close off the reactor as soon as possible. To build such a big building so fast, they cut many corners in construction. They never dreamed that the Sarcophagus would still be the only thing protecting the world from a meltdown at Chernobyl for many years to come.

By the middle of July 1986, the Chernobyl site was cleaned up enough so that plant operators could move back on to the site and prepare to start up the other three nuclear reactors which had been shut down after the accident. Naturally, people in Ukraine and around the world were frightened of the prospect of starting up three reactors that were built just like the one that had exploded. But winter was coming, and that region of the Soviet Union had few other sources of power. Without the electricity from Chernobyl, officials feared many would freeze to death. So in November, Units 1 and 2 were put back in operation. Unit 3, which had been damaged by the explosion, was repaired and back in operation by the end of the next year.

Cancer Fears

Even as the Chernobyl plant came back to life, experts debated what the full health impact of the disaster would be. One problem is that, although doctors know that radiation causes cancer, there is no way to tell whether any individual cancer victim got the disease from radiation or some other cause. Not much research had been done to learn the health impacts of small

> ### "A New Disease from Chernobyl"
> "I knew a girl, Lida by name, fourteen years old, who suffered so much because she had to wear a kerchief all the time, even when the weather was hot. She lived in Chernobyl itself and became completely bald. It is a new disease from Chernobyl and they say it has no cure. She didn't want to see her classmates; she refused to see even neighbors. She felt ashamed, but why should she?"
>
> — Emma, a Chernobyl-area resident

amounts of radiation. Some cancers take many years to show themselves.

Environmental policy in the Soviet Union was so poor that many of its citizens were exposed to many cancer-causing substances besides radiation. And the accident and evacuation caused many residents in the Chernobyl area to experience a lot of stress, which can also affect health.

Even with all the confusion, experts agree that the radiation from Chernobyl caused many cancers, particularly thyroid cancer. After the Chernobyl accident, the rate of thyroid cancer among Ukrainian children under fifteen was ten times greater than it was before the accident. What's more, sixty-four percent of children with thyroid cancer came from the most contaminated parts of the country. These facts make experts think that the rise in this type of cancer

Separate rallies in Kiev promote differing viewpoints. (left): A Ukrainian man's sign reads, "How should we live on?" He wants Chernobyl to reopen or would like other nuclear power plants built in order to provide jobs for local people. (right): A man disabled by the effects of Chernobyl protests pension cuts for victims of the catastrophe.

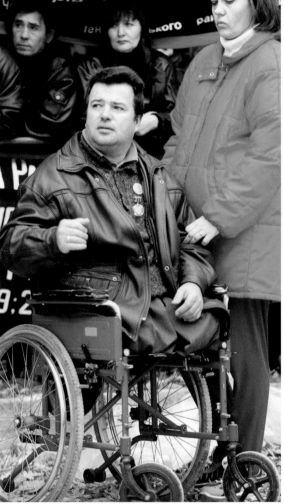

was definitely caused by radiation from the Chernobyl accident.

Increases in other types of cancer have also been reported, both in people who lived in contaminated areas and in the liquidators who cleaned up the Chernobyl site. Ukrainian nuclear experts estimate that more than two thousand five hundred deaths were caused by the disaster. But other scientists, noting that half a million people got higher radiation doses from Chernobyl, estimate the death toll at closer to five thousand.

Chernobyl has also taken its toll on the mental health of the people in the area. The fear caused by the accident itself, the stress of relocation, and the ongoing problems of poverty and uncertainty have caused an increase in mental health problems. Growing numbers of people in the Chernobyl area suffered from anxiety, depression, and other illnesses caused by mental stress.

In addition to the toll in human life, the economic costs of the Chernobyl accident have been large. Ukraine had been one of the world's largest wheat-growing regions. After the accident, huge areas of farmland in Ukraine and Belarus were so radioactive that they were taken out of production for more than ten years. Other areas cannot be used for crops for about one hundred years. And, randomly scattered "hotspots" of fallout from Chernobyl will produce radioactive crops for at least another three hundred years.

Farmers also noticed that their livestock were dying of strange diseases. The birthrate for farm animals began to drop, and many cows and sheep were born with birth defects. Among the cows that survived, milk production dropped sharply and much of the milk that was produced was too radioactive to drink.

The contamination of crops and animals caused great hardship in a region that depended so much on its farms. By 1995 — almost a decade after the accident — Ukrainian officials estimated the ongoing cost of Chernobyl at $2.3 billion a year. The government of Belarus also estimated that Chernobyl would eventually cause $235-billion worth of lost production in that country.

The Soviet Union Falls

The accident brought other big changes in the Soviet Union. Government leaders fired several top officials in the nuclear power industry.

Three major figures in the development of Communism, (left to right) Vladimir Lenin, Friedrich Engels, and Karl Marx, grace a banner in Moscow's Red Square during May Day celebrations in 1985. The Soviet Union collapsed by the end of that decade.

(Upper) Engineers of the Chernobyl nuclear power plant are shown a few moments after deactivating Reactor Number 3 on December 15, 2000.

(Right) Employees of the plant watch on a huge screen as shift chief Oleksandr Yelchishchev pulls the black switch that deactivates the last of Chernobyl's reactors.

They took authority for nuclear power away from the electric power ministry and created a new Ministry of Nuclear Power. In 1987, the director of the Chernobyl facility and his two deputies were put on trial and found guilty of "gross violations of safety regulations which led to the explosion." The three were sentenced to serve ten years in a labor camp.

Soviet authorities began to cooperate with organizations like the International Atomic Energy Agency to improve safety procedures and upgrade the design of the Chernobyl-style reactors in the Soviet Union and Eastern Europe. The Soviets dropped their plans to build more nuclear power plants and began to rely more on the country's oil and gas reserves to generate energy.

But time had run out for the Soviet government and the country's communist system. Faced with economic depression and outraged with a government full of secrecy and corruption, people in Russia, the Ukraine, and other former Soviet states staged mass protests against their rulers starting in 1989. By 1991, five years after the Chernobyl disaster, the government collapsed, and the states declared their independence. The Soviet Union was no more.

The Ukrainians had won their freedom. But they had also inherited the Chernobyl mess. The Ukrainian parliament originally planned to close all the plants at Chernobyl by 1995 and allow no more nuclear plants to be built in the country. But a shortage of power forced officials to keep Chernobyl running and even to build new nuclear plants. It was only in the year 2000, after the United States, Japan, and other industrialized nations agreed to help pay for the shutdown, that the Chernobyl reactors fell silent for good.

Outside the former Soviet Union, where radiation was less of a problem, many experts believe that Chernobyl caused few additional cancers or other health problems. But the impact on the worldwide nuclear power industry was severe. After Chernobyl, many people feared the idea of nuclear power, even though the plants built in the West were much safer.

In addition to fear, rising costs also stopped the growth of nuclear power. With new design and safety rules in place, nuclear power plants became much more expensive to build and operate. And the cost of storing spent

"I'm Used to Not Being Safe"

"What's one to do? I feel comfortable here — it's my city, my job, my life. I'm used to it not being safe."

— Lyubov Rasovova, a worker who has returned to Chernobyl

nuclear fuel was enormous. Spent fuel rods are highly radioactive and must be kept from leaking into the environment for centuries to come, even though they no longer have enough energy in them to generate power in a reactor. The technology that was supposed to produce power that was "too cheap to meter" now could not compete with plants that burned oil, coal, and gas.

Political and economic pressures caused many countries to phase out nuclear power entirely. In the United States, no new reactors have been ordered since 1978. Some plants under construction came on line, but others were never finished. And many of those already operating did not have their licenses renewed and closed down.

Energy for the Future?

Nuclear power production is declining, but the world's need for energy keeps growing. As global industry grows and the world's population climbs,

countries have a harder time filling their energy needs. But burning oil, coal, and natural gas produces carbon dioxide and other so-called "greenhouse gases" that experts say are causing global warming. Increased use of oil also forces countries like the United States to depend on foreign nations for energy.

In some areas of the U.S., the lack of power production is causing big problems. Major cities face energy shortages in peak use times. In 2001, some California cities were forced to cut power for a time to tens of thousands of residents. The state had not built a new power plant for ten years, and could not afford to buy enough outside electricity to fill the demand for power.

Also in 2001, President George W. Bush unveiled a new energy policy that called for the United States to cut its use of foreign oil. One way to it do this is to dramatically expand the use of nuclear power. Existing nuclear plants would be allowed to operate longer and produce

Alternative Energy — Any Closer?

Opponents of nuclear energy have long promoted renewable energy sources — solar, wind power, and methane gas produced from crops — as safer alternatives. Growth in these areas has been slow because renewable energy sources remain far more expensive than more traditional oil, gas, and coal plants. But with the slowed growth of nuclear power, energy companies have invested more money in researching renewable sources. The U.S. Department of Energy predicts that by 2020, about ten percent of the nation's energy needs will be met with renewable sources — almost as much as that provided by nuclear power.

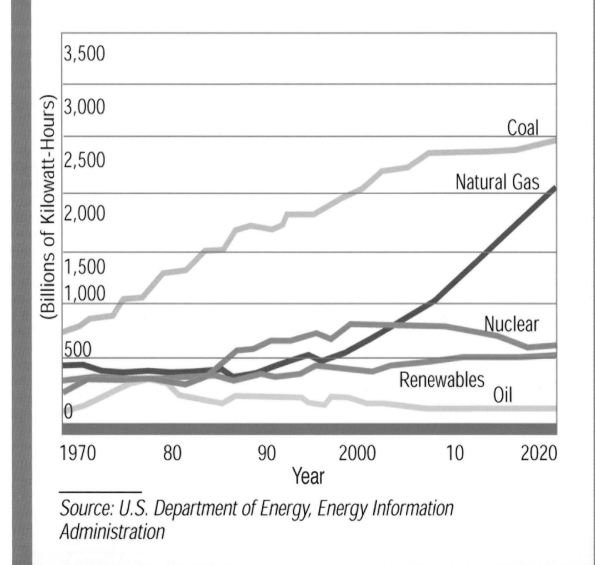

Electricity Generation by Fuel: Current Trends

(Billions of Kilowatt-Hours)

3,500
3,000
2,500
2,000
1,500
1,000
500
0

Coal

Natural Gas

Nuclear

Renewables

Oil

1970   80   90   2000   10   2020

Year

Source: U.S. Department of Energy, Energy Information Administration

more power per plant than originally allowed. In addition, the United States would support the development of new, safer designs for nuclear power plants. Some people praised the president's energy policy for dealing with the tough issues facing America's future energy needs. But the provision for increased nuclear power set off protests from those who feel the country should be developing renewable energy sources like solar and wind power.

While the industrial nations debate their energy future, inside Chernobyl's Exclusion Zone all is quiet. Other than official visitors and plant workers, no one is allowed to enter The Zone, much less live there. In the once-thriving town

The Chernobyl area was once bustling with people, activities, laughter, and life. Now, ghost towns sprinkle a silent landscape.

An abandoned schoolroom provides an obvious example of Chernobyl's enormous impact on everyday life. Friendships were broken, educational opportunities were lost, and lives were changed forever as people scattered during the evacuation.

"Chernobyl
Still Casts a Shadow"
"Chernobyl . . . still casts a shadow over millions of Russians. It is government's sacred duty to ensure safety from radiation and rule out any repeat of the Chernobyl nightmare."

— Russian President Vladimir Putin, in a 2000 speech marking the fourteenth anniversary of the Chernobyl disaster.

of Pripyat, the streets are deserted. The only residents are packs of wild dogs, descendants of the pets abandoned by their masters after the accident. Pripyat will remain a ghost town until the levels of radioactivity have dropped to safe levels.

Scientists predict that "The Zone" will be safe for life again in about three hundred years.

Time Line

1970	Work begins on the Chernobyl nuclear facility.
1979	Secret document warns Soviet leaders of dangerous design flaws in the Chernobyl reactors.
1986	April 25: Technicians begin a test of the Chernobyl Unit 4 reactor.
	April 26: Unit 4 explodes, destroying the reactor and releasing a plume of radioactivity into the air.
	April 27: Authorities begin to evacuate people from Pripyat, near the Chernobyl plant.
	April 28: Swedish nuclear authorities detect radioactive fallout coming from the Soviet Union.
	April 30: Soviets reveal first details of the Chernobyl accident to world.
	May 3: Evacuation of 75,000 people living within a 19-mile (30-km) radius of Chernobyl begins.
	May 9: Firefighters finally extinguish the graphite fire in the reactor.
	November: a 300,000-ton (272,000-tonne) containment building around Unit 4, is completed. Chernobyl Units 1 and 2 return to operation.
1987	December: Chernobyl Unit 3 returns to operation.
1991	Soviet Union falls; Ukraine and Belarus become independent nations.
1996	Industrialized nations agree to help Ukraine shut down the reactors at Chernobyl.
2000	Unit 3 — Chernobyl's last reactor — is shut down.

Glossary

cesium 137 a radioactive isotope of cesium with a half-life of thirty years; produced by a nuclear reactor or by detonation of a nuclear weapon. Cesium 137 fallout from Chernobyl may cause about one thousand extra cases of cancer.

China Syndrome an event in which the fuel rods in a nuclear reactor melt down and burn through the reactor floor.

core the part of a nuclear reactor where the nuclear reaction occurs.

DNA abbreviation for deoxyribonucleic acid, a complex molecule found in the nucleus of most cells, which tells the cells how to divide and create organs.

fission a chain reaction in which the neutrons given off by radioactive atoms split other atoms, causing them to give off more neutrons which split other atoms.

fuel rod a rod of radioactive material, usually uranium, used in the core of a nuclear reactor.

Geiger counter a device that measures the radioactivity of an area or object.

graphite a dense form of carbon that absorbs radioactive particles. Graphite rods help control the fission process in a nuclear reactor.

greenhouse gas a gas, such as carbon dioxide, that causes Earth's atmosphere to trap heat; produced by burning fossil fuels such as coal, gas, and oil.

iodine an element used by the thyroid gland to produce hormones that control energy use and growth; radioactive fallout often contains a radioactive form of iodine that causes thyroid cancer.

isotope a form of an element that is slightly different from its parent element; it has most of the characteristics of the pure element, but may differ in properties such as radioactivity and physical state (liquid, gas, or solid).

lethal deadly.

liquidator a person who worked to fight fires or clean up the Chernobyl nuclear power plant after the explosion.

meltdown an event in which the fuel rods in a nuclear reactor overheat and begin to melt together.

mutation changes in DNA, that cause deformed or abnormal growth.

plutonium a highly radioactive element produced by the fission of uranium; can be used to make nuclear weapons.

radiation energy or particles given off by unstable atoms as they break down.

radioactive (a substance or object that gives off radiation.

reactor the core of a nuclear power plant where the fission reaction takes place.

Sarcophagus the massive concrete structure built to contain the ruins of the Chernobyl nuclear power plant; also used to refer to any stone coffin.

Soviet Union the Union of Soviet Socialist Republics (U.S.S.R.), a communist nation that collapsed in 1991.

strontium 90 an isotope of strontium with a half-life of twenty-nine years; produced in nuclear reactors or from detonation of nuclear weapons; behaves like calcium in the body, where it settles in the bones and teeth.

thyroid a gland at the front of the neck that secretes hormones for controlling the growth and energy use of an organism.

turbine a device that generates electricity when it spins.

uranium the first radioactive element that was discovered. It is used as fuel in a nuclear reactor.

For More Information

Books

Chernobyl. World Disasters (series) Don Nardo (Lucent)

Meltdown: A Race against Nuclear Disaster at Three Mile Island: A Reporter's Story.
    Wilborn Hampton (Candlewick Press)

Nuclear Disaster at Chernobyl. Take Ten: Disaster (series). Robin Cruise (Artesian Press)

Phoenix Rising (Fiction). Karen Hesse (Penguin Putnam)

Quarks and Sparks: The Story of Nuclear Power. Science and Society (series).
    J. S. Kidd (Facts on File)

Videos

The American Experience: Meltdown at Three Mile Island. (PBS Home Video)

The China Syndrome. (Fiction) (Columbia/Tristar)

NOVA: Back to Chernobyl. (Vestron)

Nuclear Rescue 911: Broken Arrows & Incidents. (Goldhil Home Media)

Web Sites

Chernobyl: Assessment of Radiological and Health Impacts
www.nea.fr/html/rp/chernobyl/chernobyl.html

Chernobyl Nuclear Disaster
www.chernobyl.co.uk

Chernobyl Children's Project
www.adiccp.org

United Nations, Chernobyl Disaster
www.un.org/ha/chernobyl

Nuclear Energy Institute Science Club
www.nrc.gov/reading-rm/basic-ref/students.html

Index

Index (continued)